Permission to Laugh

Permission to Laugh

My Favourite Funny Stories

Clive Dunn

Illustrations by Jessica Dunn

★

Michael O'Mara Books Limited

First published in Great Britain in 1996 by
Michael O'Mara Books Limited
9 Lion Yard
Tremadoc Road
London SW4 7NQ

A CIP catalogue record for this book is available from the
British Library

ISBN 1-85479-220-2

1 3 5 7 9 10 8 6 4 2

Designed and typeset by K DESIGN, Winscombe, Somerset
Printed in England by Clays Ltd, St Ives plc

*I dedicate this book to my
five-month-old granddaughter Alice
– who is almost as childish as her
grandfather!*

★

Dear Ladies and Gentlemen

Welcome! And thank you for asking for permission to laugh at my favourite funny stories.

These pages contain material gleaned by me over the last sixty years to entertain people who like a bit of fun.

Herein you will find ancient and modern 'patter' and jokes used by my grandfather Frank Lynne, my mother Connie Clive, my father Bobby Dunn, and myself. So here we go – over a hundred and twenty years of my family battling with audiences, dodging tomatoes and anything else that was in season.

Too many funny stories taken at once can be indigestible – one or two after meals is ideal.

If you read these to an audience of friends, speak up and use the appropriate funny accent. If you find this difficult, try reading with your trousers down, then people might not notice how bad the joke is.

Never allow anyone to 'top' your joke – that is, start another story before the laughter has 'died'. If they try, an aggressive 'SHUSH' should suffice but if they persist, try a well-aimed head butt. Then, while their eyes are watering, you can start off with your next little gem.

It is quite possible to dominate the public in a public house or the diners at a dinner party for an entire evening with that method. If you are dining with royalty, it is probably better to use the head butt sparingly. The determined joke teller should be able to get through his entire life without ever having to have a conversation.

Rude-word-hating adults, children and small people are protected in this book by this sign:

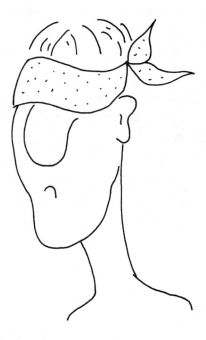

When they come across it, they should immediately blindfold themselves before reading the next joke.

All comedians steal jokes from each other, even though they won't admit it. So, jokers of the world, unite – you filthy swine.

I want to thank all the dear friends and enemies who contributed to these writings, but I don't think I will. We don't want to involve them in expensive law suits do we?

Remember:

NONE OF THESE JOKES HAVE BEEN TESTED ON ANIMALS BY CHILDREN.

So here we go again.

Love and multiply

Yours
celine x. x .

P.S. Read on if you dare! As Cpl. Jones might say . . . 'You have permission to laugh.'

Music-Hall

After being released from the army not long after the end of World War II, I was asked to do some turns at the Players Theatre Club near Charing Cross, London. Victorian Music-Hall was always on the menu. When I did one act my pay was six pounds a week. If I did two acts I was paid eight pounds a week and every night a free sandwich and a cup of coffee.

On and off for some years I enjoyed working at this jolly little venue until I discovered that the washer-upper in the restaurant was being paid twelve pounds a week. I concluded that the washer-upper's washing-up was funnier than my act.

P.S. The washer-upper's name was Les Dawson.

Old Time Music-Hall

Some time ago, I was performing in an 'Old Time Music-Hall' show, and I couldn't get the audience to sing the rather complicated chorus, so I gave up and said, 'Ladies and Gentlemen, I'd like to tell you a little historical story.' And a rather sloshed voice in the back row said, 'Must you?'

I said, 'I'll tell you this little historical story. In Ancient Rome with the fountains playing, and the nude maidens dancing round the fountains. . .'

And the voice from the back said, 'They don't y'know.'

I repeated, 'In Ancient Rome with the fountains playing, and the nude maidens dancing round and round the fountains. . .'

And again the voice said, 'They don't y'know.'

I said, 'Why, were you ever in Ancient Rome?'

He said, 'Sorry, I thought you said Edgware Road.'

STAGE DIRECTIONS: *Knees slightly bent and up and down as if trotting.*

Two mounted police were chatting one day as they trotted back to the stables. The brighter one said, 'You've been looking down in the dumps recently. What's the matter?'

'Well, I'm not having much fun with the wife these days. She doesn't seem interested.'

His mate pondered a while, and said, 'Well, when you go home tonight, get that old gypsy feeling back. Just walk in, slam your lunch bag down on the hall stand, don't bother to take your boots off, grab the missis, and do it on the mat in front of the fire. Get that old gypsy feeling back again!'

The next day on duty the bright one said to his mate, 'Well, how did you get on?'

His mate said, *'Not bad – gave the kids a good laugh.'*

A life on the Ocean

In the 1920s and 30s, Britain was famous for its seaside summer shows. Sometimes called 'concert parties', they were to be found in small wooden theatres on a pier, or very very near the sea.

When the summer season was over, we'd all go back to London and try to get into West End shows.

Here's a typical interview:

STAGE DIRECTIONS: *The interviewee should wear a monocle and funny hat and a blazer.*

West End manager said to the concert party performer, 'Where have you been performing?'

He said, 'I've been with the Merry Magnets, a nice little concert party, down by the sea. The best place to have a seaside show is near the sea.'

'How was business, did you do good business?'

'Oh no no, . . . not at all, no we did rather badly. Actually, we got rather hungry. I got so hungry I had to eat my understudy. He was a bit gritty. Mind you, it's not surprising . . . *He was a sand dancer.*

16

'And then disaster befell us. One night we were doing the show, and an enormous wave swept right over the pier.'

'Good heavens! What happened to you?'

'I floated out of the window and my wife accompanied me on the piano.'

The Audition

STAGE DIRECTIONS: *Get a close friend to read this with you. Have a few drinks then decide which of you is going to be the simple person who wants to be a megastar. He should use a northern accent to give him some confidence – something to hang on to, as we say.*

AGENT: Good afternoon.

SIMPLE: Thank you very much.

AGENT: And what do you do?

SIMPLE: (*Thinking hard*) When?

AGENT: I mean – what do you do when you're performing?

SIMPLE: Well, it depends on what sort of part it is. If it's a scornful part, sometimes for instance I look this way, or another time I look that way – I usually like to have my knees slightly bent so that the audience knows I am ready for anything.

AGENT: (*Trying to be polite*) Yes well – do you sing?

SIMPLE: Yes.

AGENT: What do you sing?

SIMPLE: Songs mostly.

AGENT: No, I mean how do you sing?

SIMPLE: I just open my mouth and out it pops!

AGENT: No, no, do you sing soprano or contralto?

SIMPLE: (*Slightly puzzled*) Yes.

AGENT: Yes what?

SIMPLE: Yes please?

AGENT: Oh dear – what else do you do?

SIMPLE: I write songs.

AGENT: You write songs?

SIMPLE: Yes, whenever I hear a good song, I go home and write it. I wrote the Beatles.

AGENT: YOU wrote the Beatles. What about 'Yesterday'? I suppose you wrote that?

SIMPLE: No, I'm writing that tomorrow.

AGENT I think I've got the right job for you.

SIMPLE: Oo er!

AGENT: Pardon.

SIMPLE: I said, 'Oo er.'

AGENT: There's a circus coming to town next week. They need someone to put their head in the lion's mouth.

SIMPLE: I wouldn't like that.

AGENT: Why not?

SIMPLE: I'd worry.

AGENT: There's no need to worry. This lion hasn't got any teeth.

SIMPLE: I don't want to be gummed to death!

AGENT: (*Shaking hands*) Goodbye, forever!

★Grandma Dunn

STAGE DIRECTIONS: *Read this quietly and with reverence.*

When my old granny thought her last days were coming she called all the family round. And we all stood round her bed and looked down at this little white face. She said:

'Well, boys and girls – I've had a good life, and when I go I want plenty of cars and plenty of flowers. I want you and uncle Bertie in the first car, I want Mary and 'er lot in the second car, and Jimmy's family with all 'ers in the last car. I want you to drive up the high street, round by the kids' playground, through the market place, stop outside The Dog and Duck, an' all go in an' 'ave a nice drink – and leave me outside like you always bloody well do!'

IN THE SPRING

So I said to the landlady's daughter, . . .
I'm feeling full of fun,
Any chance of a bit of whoopie?
She said . . . Sorry, it's Lent.
What a funny answer!

Bonjour

STAGE DIRECTIONS: *Wear a monocle and water wings while reading this story.*

I still can't believe there's a tunnel between England and France. However, there is. I don't use it, but people do I believe. I prefer to sail.

We sailed across there the other day. It was beautiful. The sun was shining and the waves were waving.

And there I stood on the poop. Well not on the poop, you wouldn't want to stand on a thing like that.

When we nearly got to France, the poor little craft foundered on a sort of sandbank. I rolled up my jodhpurs and paddled ashore.

A little French Gallic Gaul came running up to me and said, 'Monsieur, you'd like a nice blonde lady?'

I said, 'No, I want the Harbour Master.'

He said, 'Very difficult, but I'll try.'

Rex Jameson

Rex Jameson, one of my very favourite comedians, played a character called Mrs Shufflewick – a drunken old tart, full of charm and booze. He would stagger out on to the stage and say:

'Hello dears, what d'you think of this? (waving a feather boa). Untouched pussy, very rare in London at the moment – Ooh I had a terrible night last night. I was in this pub and I had three large gins, two pints of Guinness, a large Port, a double Benedictine and a pork pie, and when they chucked us out, I was as sick as a dog. *I don't think that pork pie agreed with me!*

'I thought, well, I'm not very well, I'll go home, and so as not to wake the old man, I'll take me clothes off at the bottom of the stairs, and just creep up. And when I got to the bend at the top of the stairs, *I found I was on a '92' bus!*'

And so he went on – very rude and with perfect timing. Poor old Rex has gone beyond the stars now, but I'm sure he won't mind me quoting a one-off joke he did on Boat Race night. Oxford had just won the Boat Race, and Rex had celebrated. He drifted on to the stage, and said:

'I was asked by the manager of the Boat Race to go down and kiss the cox of the winning crew. Naturally I refused. I've never even been introduced to the fella! I don't mind stroking them under Putney Bridge, but I mean, you've got sixteen oars and only twenty minutes to do it in!'

I wouldn't have missed that for the world.

Title of an Ancient Song

You can't keep a horse in a lighthouse.

Ma' in Law

STAGE DIRECTIONS: *While reading this story, wear narrow black trousers and a small hat.*

As soon as we know my mother-in-law's going to visit, everybody looks miserable. Even the poor little dog looks miserable. Mind you – it's not surprising about him, I had his tail cut off this morning. I want to make sure when she arrives that *nobody gives her a welcome*!

The best part of my mother-in-law's visit, is seeing her off at the railway station. But doesn't it make your hands black, *patting the engine*?

We gave her a rough time last visit. She had to go off and see the doctor. She said to the doctor, 'I don't feel so good.'

He said, 'You don't look so good. You'd better have an examination. Go up to room number three. You'll see some men in white there, take your clothes off, lie on the operating table, I'll be up in a minute.'

She goes upstairs, takes her clothes off, lies on the operating table, been there about five minutes, sits up and says, 'Well, isn't someone going to do something?'

And one of the men in white said, 'Well lady, if you'll get dressed and go home, we can get on with painting the room.'

When the doctor arrived eventually, he examined her and said, 'You've got acute appendicitis.'

She said, 'Thank you, but I came to be examined not admired.'

He said, 'A woman with your skin condition needs a special treatment. When you go to bed at night smother yourself in goose grease.'

She said, 'I've tried that but the old man keeps sliding out of bed.'

He said, 'Well, river water's very good. Try a daily swim in the river.' So the first day she went down to the river, took her clothes off once again, and started to swim gingerly up and down the river. She looked up on the bank and there's a young man sitting beside her clothes. Rather panicky she said, 'Would you mind getting away from my clothes, I've no bathing costume on, I'd like to come out and get dressed.'

And the young man just stared at her.

She said, 'Young man, would you get away from my clothes, I've no bathing costume on, I want to come out and get dressed.'

Still no answer. In desperation she searched round in the water for something with which to cover herself, reached down, and found an old frying pan, put it in front of herself, went boldly out of the water and as she got to the young man she said, 'You know what I think don't you?'

He said, 'Yes – You think there's a bottom to that frying pan!'

Dublin

STAGE DIRECTIONS: *Use Kerry accent.*

The explorers' association had organised a trip to the Antarctic. The head of the expedition was asked to phone back every four hours to report on progress.

After several days a voice phoned through to headquarters. Headquarters said, 'How's the expedition going?'

The voice said, 'Not at all well. In fact, very very bad. We've lost six of our best huskies, the main sledge has splintered right down the centre and we can't use it, and to make matters much much worse, the expedition doctor has fallen down a crevice and we can't get him out – but things are bound to improve once we get out of Dublin.'

Hamming it up?

Leonard Sachs, the well-known music-hall chairman, took his entire family to see the film *Around the World in Eighty Days*.

Robert Newton was one of the stars in the film and he was working his arse off as usual. To put it politely he was overacting.

It was a long film and in the interval Leonard Sachs's mother said to him, 'Leonard, was Robert Newton alive when they made this film?'

Old Fashioned Patter

STAGE DIRECTIONS: *With monocle and a straw hat.*

I once went for a short holiday to Brighton. Unfortunately, a political conference was going on and I couldn't find anywhere to stay.

I wandered about, up and down the promenade, went to every hotel, and I couldn't find anywhere to rest my head. Then eventually, I wandered over the road towards the sea, and I heard a voice crying in distress.

'Help, help, I'm drowning!'

(I knew it was a cry of distress by the wording).

I ran bravely to the edge of the water and said, 'What's that?'

And the voice said, 'Heeelp, I'm drowning.'

I said, 'Could you tell me your name please?'

She said, 'I'm Miss Brown, heeelp, I'm drowning!'

I said, 'Where are you staying Miss Brown?'

She said, 'I'm staying at The Metropole . . . lapol . . . pulol . . . blob . . . bullob. . . .' So I went straight off to The Metropole, knocked on the door, and Mrs Metronome came to the door . . . she was a funny little woman . . . kept going from side to side.

I said, 'Have you a Miss Brown staying here?'

She said, 'Yes.'

I said, 'Could I have her room please?'

She said, *'Sorry, I've just let it to the gentleman who pushed her in!'*

So I strolled disconsolately away on to the promenade, and tried to get on a bus. And a man in front of me tried to get on the same bus with a very large dog. The conductor said, 'You can't come on this bus with that dog.'

He said, 'I can come on that bus with this dog.'

He said, 'You can't come on this bus with that dog.'

He said, 'Why can't I come on that bus with this dog?'

He said, 'Because it's too big.'

And the man said, 'Well, you know what you can do with the bus, don't you?'

And the conductor said, *'Well if you can do the same with the dog you can come on the bus!'*

So I got on the bus, and I'd been sitting there a little while, when I noticed a young lady stroking a pussy cat.

I said, 'Ho ho, . . . I wish I were that cat.'

She said, *'I bet you don't. I'm taking it to the vet's.'*

And the man next to her took out a drawing pad, and looking closely at me started to draw. Rather embarrassed I said, 'I see you're an artist.'

He said, 'Not exactly Sir, *I design door knockers.*'

So I went on the top of the bus in rather a huff and noticed two ladies sitting in front of me, and one of them said, 'What a panorama.'

And the other one said, '*I can't smell anything!*'

And the other lady said, 'Oh, let's go to the pictures tonight. What's on?'

Her friend said, '*Moby Dick.*'

The other one said, 'Oh, I don't like those sex films!'

She said, 'It's not a sex film, . . . it's about whales.'

She said, 'Well, I don't like the Welsh either!'

Well, I can't stand ignorant people, so I went downstairs to get away from them.

And the bus stopped at a bus queue and the conductor looked out and said, 'Hurry along please.'

And a young girl at the back of the queue said, 'Can I come on in front of the others, I'm pregnant.'

He said, 'Certainly, stand back Ladies and Gentlemen, let the pregnant lady on please.'

On the bus, the conductor said to a man, 'Will you please stand up Sir, and let the lady be seated. She's pregnant.'

And he said to the girl, 'How long have you been that way?'

She said, '*Half an hour . . . doesn't it make you tired.*'

(Wait For Applause, None Forthcoming, Retire In Confusion.)

Funny Friends

Somehow, things seem twice as funny when they happen to your friends and relations!

★ ★ ★

Top Billing

Dear Hattie Jacques, the plump and beautiful star of the 'Carry On' films, was on tour. She hated being overweight and was always slimming. When the touring show reached Hereford she went straight to the theatre and went round the front to see the billing – which read in large letters:

'TONIGHT. HATTIE JACQUES. ALL-IN WRESTLING'

Grandma Jacques

Hattie once told me that her mother and grandmother were shopping in Bond Street, London, in the middle of August.

Later they were looking for a bus to take them home to Earls Court, when they found themselves outside the hotel where millionaires and sometimes royalty stay. The famous Claridges.

Hattie's grandma was fanning herself, and the very very posh top-hatted commissionaire rather patronisingly said to her, 'Good afternoon Madam.'

She said, 'Good afternoon – How's business?'

He said, 'It's rather quiet as a matter of fact.'

She said, 'What do you expect in a side street!'

My Mother; Connie Clive

When my mother was ninety-odd, I took her to the Lyric Theatre, Hammersmith, to see John Le Mesurier and Constance Cummings in *Hay Fever*. In the interval, I was reading the programme notes written by Sheridan Morley.

I said to my mother: 'Look at this, it says Noël Coward wrote *Hay Fever* in three days.'

She said, 'He should've taken four.'

John Le Mesurier

I was with my old friend John Le Mesurier in Trafalgar Square one New Year's Eve. Everybody cheering and laughing and falling in the pond.

John went up to a constable and said, 'Excuse me, could you tell me where I can find Alcoholics Anonymous?'

The police officer said, 'Why Sir, do you want to join?'

And John said, 'No – I want to resign.'

Arthur Lowe

Dear Arthur Lowe, alias Captain Mainwaring, one day decided he wanted to drive my ancient butcher's van. 'I'll take over the wheel,' he said.

Driving near a farm he managed to run over a large cockerel.

Being a perfect gentleman, he picked the cockerel up, knocked on the farmer's door and said, 'I'm sorry my man, I'd like to replace your cockerel.'

And the farmer said, 'Please yourself – the hens are round the back.'

Terry Thomas could never get to the end of this story without breaking up with laughter.

Three soldiers in a field hospital were visited by a general who said to the first, 'What's wrong with you?' The soldier said, 'Nasty infection round the back part Sir, the treatment is a stiff bristle brush and a bucket of hot soapy water.' The general said, 'And what is your ambition now?' The man said, 'To get better then back to the trenches to fight gerry Sir!' 'Very good,' said the general, 'and what about you, private?'

'Well Sir, I've a nasty attack of piles Sir and my treatment is a stiff bristle brush with a bucket of hot soapy water.' 'Your ambition?' said the general. 'To get back to the front Sir and fight the enemy Sir.'

'Excellent,' said the general, 'and you, what are you here for?' The third man said, 'I've got a mouth and gum infection and tonsillitis Sir.'

'What treatment are you expecting?' said the general.

'A stiff bristle brush and a bucket of hot soapy water Sir,' said the man. The general said, 'What's your ambition?' The soldier said, 'I want to get the stiff bristle brush before the others do Sir.'

Tommy the Great

I once did a nine-month stint with Tommy Cooper at that fun factory known as the London Palladium.

We did twice daily performances, and three on Saturday.

Tommy, who used to escape to his home in Eastbourne on Sundays, was obliged to sit around with well-intentioned neighbours after dinner to watch some of his television shows. Being Tommy, he'd rather've been out having a tumble down the sink (*drink*).

One particular sketch involved a few plumbers, where they spent nearly ten minutes splashing around in water, eventually with water up to their waists.

While they were watching this sketch, one of the neighbours who had never cracked a smile during the whole performance, said to Tommy, 'Was that real water?'

Ronnie Corbett

Ronnie Corbett said to me that he'd been offered a part in a sketch which involved a bit of ballet dancing.

He'd never done such a thing before.

So he went and bought some very expensive tights, put them on, and went into his study to have a practice, and with great difficulty, put his foot up on the mantelpiece, and the dog went for him.

He said, 'Well he loves all those little chunky bits.'

The next day he went to rehearsals, changed into the tights, walked into the rehearsal room, and one of the actors said, 'Ron, what a funny place to keep your holiday money.'

Travel with the Famous

One of the last funny things Dickie Henderson ever told me was this . . .

Eric Sykes went on holiday to Kenya with Sir John and Lady Mills. They all got a dose of the Kenya trots even before they got off the plane!

The next day, they were taken to a Masai village to watch the villagers building a house.

Eric Sykes said, 'I wish I'd been here yesterday, I could've helped them make the roof.'

And Lady Mills said, 'We should all have been here and we could've built a block of flats.'

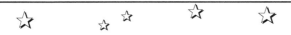

Dangerous Stories

Dangerous Stories

People of a sensitive disposition are advised to wear wellington boots and protective clothing during the next few draughty passages.

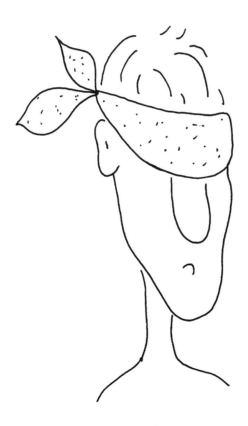

Fussy

There were two geologists working in the Brazilian jungle, hoping to find some minerals. And one of them said, 'Isn't it strange we haven't been bothered by any wild animals. We've had no trouble at all!'

And the other man said, 'Well, we probably smell so much, the animals won't come near us. We haven't had a bath for weeks. Let's go down to the river and freshen up a bit.'

And when they got to the river, as they were stripping off, one of them noticed that the other one'd got very thin through not eating well in the jungle. He said, 'There's a big gap between your trouser top and your tummy!'

Just as he said that a snake fell out of a branch, down into the gentleman's trousers. He saw what he thought was another snake and they had a fight.

And the snake who fell out of the tree was the winner.

The man was in agony, bitten by a poisonous snake, he shouted to his friend, 'Get back to the radio, phone the doctor, and ask him what we can do, QUICK, QUICK.'

The other man ran back, got on the radio, told the doctor what happened, and the doctor said:

'He could die! If you don't get back there quickly and suck the poison out, he will die.'

So he ran back to his friend, who gasped:

'What did the doctor say?'

He said, 'You're gonna die!'

A Lot of them About

A man bought four new golf balls and put them in his trouser pocket in a rush to catch the bus. Then, on the bus he had to stand, the bus was so full. And the balls in his pocket started to jiggle about. A girl sitting near him gazed in that direction absolutely fascinated.

The man noticed the direction of her eyes and said, 'It's all right – only golf balls.'

She said, 'Oh dear! Is it anything like tennis elbow?'

Ploughman's Lunch

The landlord of a pub is very interested in the sexual exploits of his customers. And he asked a young guy:

'Fred, how often do you do it?'

He said, 'Well, I've only been married two weeks . . . about twelve times a week!'

'George, how often do you do it?'

He said, 'Well, I've been married a couple o'years, . . . twice a week I 'spose.'

There was a very very ancient man in the corner of the pub, sipping cider, and the landlord said, 'Jasper, how often d'you do it?'

He said, 'Every anniversary, . . . it's next Thursday and I'm not looking forward to it a bit!'

Short Shrift

A gentleman went to a penis enlargement clinic for obvious reasons.

He was told the price.

Five thousand for an Anglo-Saxon type, eight thousand for a Mediterranean type and twelve thousand for a Caribbean type.

The anxious man said, 'I'll have to ask the wife – I'll go and phone home.'

When he came back the doctor said, 'What did she say?'

He said, 'She says she'd sooner have a new kitchen!'

Circa 1923.

A woman was had up in court for having an affair with a dog.

The sentence was – The dog should have his licence taken away from him.

A woman at the back of the court said:

'She should have the cat!'

And the judge fainted.

Golf

While searching for an errant ball,
through mossy woods and banks,
I trod upon an old man's arse
And a female voice said, 'Thanks!'

Change of Direction

A man went out on a blind date.

They had dinner and then got up to dance. They danced smoochily for quite a while, and he suddenly said, 'Can I take you home to bed?'

She said, 'No – I'm a lesbian. Y'know what I'd really like?'

He said, 'No.'

She said, 'I'd like to take that beautiful black singer to bed with me. Swing us round and look at her and you'll see why.'

They swung around, and he gazed at the beautiful black singer and burst into tears.

She said, 'What's the matter?'

He said, 'I think I'm a lesbian too!'

★ ★ ★

On and Off

In a small hick town in the Australian outback the guests were gathering for the wedding ceremony and festivities. Suddenly the white-faced father of the bride announced, 'Sorry mates, the whole thing's off. We've lost the key to the booze cupboard and the best man's just had it off with the bride.' The whole company was devastated and retired en masse to the local bar.

An hour later, the bride's father appeared once again – 'It's OK folks the whole thing's on again. We've found the key to the drinks cupboard and the best man's apologised!'

Musical

A little boy was playing truant just outside the school, hiding under some bushes. He was pretending to play the drums on some Coca-Cola tins, when a little girl saw him and said:

'What'you doing?'

He said, 'I'm a drummer.'

She said, 'Ooh, I like drummers, giv'us a kiss.'

So he did so.

She lifted up her little skirt and said, 'Would you like to kiss me there?'

He said, 'No thanks, . . . I'm not a real drummer.'

Personally Speaking

Speaking as a veteran of World War II, I've found that so-called 'gay people' make brave and reliable soldiers so the idea of them being banned from the armed services must be the biggest joke of the century.

Hence . . .

RECRUITING OFFICER: *(To applicant)* Are you Gay?

APPLICANT: Not exactly Sir, I just help them out when they're busy.

The Shrink

A man of eighty imagines he's got some psychiatric problems about sex.

He's worried because he can only make love three times a night. When he tells the psychiatrist this, the psychiatrist says, 'Well, I'm thirty-eight and I can only make love twice a night.'

And the old man says, *'I'm not interested in your problems.'*

Fancy

A gay man went to a fancy dress party, dressed as a pirate, with a parrot on his shoulder.

He fancied one of the other guests and said:

'If you can guess what this is on my shoulder, you can take me home.'

The man said, 'An elephant!'

So he said, 'Oh well, . . . that's near enough!'

Changing Guard

During the ceremony of the Changing of the Guard at Buckingham Palace, a man said to a very pregnant lady, 'It's a pity the little fella can't see the Changing of the Guard.'

She said, 'It's all right, I've taken me knickers off, . . . he can hear the band.'

The Lighthouse Keeper's Diary

January 9th, 1920
Midnight. Force ten gale.
Ran up the stairs a bit sharpish
and screwed meself to the roof.

There's no Business...

There's no Business . . .

Standing on the pavement, watching a travelling circus parade through the town, an onlooker spotted an old army comrade with a bucket and spade. He was following the elephants and cleaning up after them. He called his old friend over and said, 'My dear old mate. What a comedown for a regimental sergeant major! How much do they pay you?'

The man said, 'Five pounds a day.'

His friend said, 'I can offer you £250-a-week in my factory – put down the elephant droppings – come work for me.'

And the man said, 'What, and give up show business?'

How's Business?

I did a Sunday night concert in Hereford once. There'd been a bit of a muddle, there was only one man sitting in the back of the stalls. That was the audience! So I had a chat with my friends, and went on and announced, 'Good evening Sir, although you are on your own tonight, we're going to perform the concert for you from beginning to end as if the theatre was full.'

And the old man stood up and shouted, 'Well, don't take too long – I'm waiting to lock up!'

Understandable

A travelling circus manager lost his star attraction one day, the trapeze act had walked out on him. He advertised for a new top of the bill.

A day later an agent arrived with a very muscly, tough-looking bald-headed acrobat.

The manager said, 'What does he do?'

And the agent replied: 'He'll climb up that sixty-foot tower, and dive — '

'I know,' said the manager, 'we've seen it before, he dives into a flaming bath of petrol.'

'No he doesn't,' said the agent. 'The man dives straight on to the sawdust, on his head.'

'Let's see him,' said the manager. 'If he can do it I'll give him five hundred pounds a week.'

The agent gave the acrobat the nod, and he climbed up the sixty-foot tower, waved, bowed, landed on his head in the ring, stood up, staggered around and waited. Then the manager said, 'That's a sensation. Offer him five hundred pounds a week. Does he speak English?'

The agent said, 'No, leave it to me.'

He went up to the acrobat, whispered in his ear,

and the acrobat shook his head.

He came back and told the manager, 'He won't accept.'

The manager said, 'Well, it's a sensational act, and I have to have somebody, so offer him seven fifty.'

The agent went up and whispered in the man's ear again. He got another shake of the head.

He went back to the manager and said, 'He won't accept.'

And the manager said, 'Well, offer him one thousand pounds a week and that's my final offer.'

The agent went back and whispered yet again into the acrobat's ear.

He got another shake of the head. He went back and told the manager, 'He won't accept it.'

'Why not?' said the manager.

The agent said, *'Well, he says he's never done it before, and he doesn't like it!'*

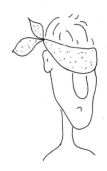

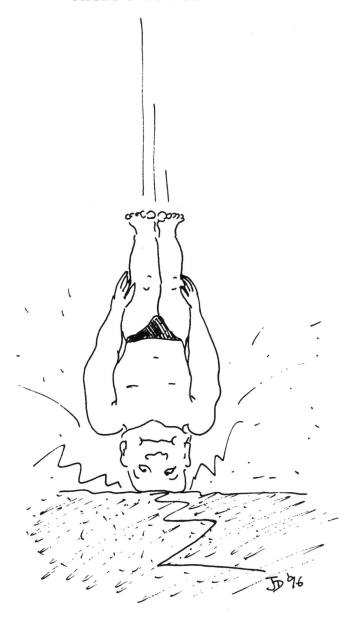

Small Part

Actors often spend months waiting for the phone to ring with an offer of work. The poor dear I refer to had been waiting for nearly nine years.

He was watching television in his miserable bed-sitter when suddenly the phone rang. He jumped up and the voice said, 'Hurry, it's James, company manager at the Queen's Theatre, Shaftesbury Avenue. Quick John, jump in a cab and come up. Someone has been taken ill. There's just one very important line – "Hark, I hear the cannons roar." We'll pay the cab and a hundred pounds. Get us out of trouble please!'

John in a panic said, 'I can't matey. I'm too nervous, haven't worked for years.'

James implored him, 'Please – do it for us, quick, one line: "Hark, I hear the cannons roar."'

'OK, OK,' said the actor.

All the way up to the theatre in the cab he practised, 'Hark, I hear the cannons roar,' with every different intonation, in every different way.

On arriving at the stage door, the stage manager

threw a cloak and hat on him, shouting, 'Quick – you're on.'

As he ran on the stage, there was an enormous explosion. He said, *'What the fuck was that!'*

Thin Ice

In one of the very many European International skating competitions, Andrew Murphy was announced, and he flew at a terrific speed into the middle of the ice rink, did a marvellous pirouette, and fell flat on his back.

Smilingly, he got up, made a brave dash round the rink, inside edge, outside edge, wallop, flat on his back again.

He got up, bravely, and whizzed round the rink for seven minutes.

He made twenty-two errors.

The marks came up. UK gave him 1.5, Norway 2, Italy 1, France 0.5, Sweden 1.5, Ireland 9.5.

The chief referee came over and said to the Irish judge, 'That was a bit generous wasn't it?'

And the Kerry man said, 'Well, don't forget – it is pretty slippery out there.'

Let's be Frank

During a stage production of *Anne Frank*, the actress playing the name part was giving such a bad performance, that when the Gestapo arrived to search the house, someone in the audience shouted, 'She's in the attic!'

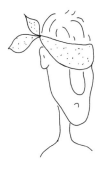

Old Wives' Tale

An actress friend of mine who had had a spot of bad luck – she'd been out of work for twelve years – found it necessary to get a job travelling round the country for a family planning company.

She had been told to knock on doors and ask what method of contraception the people in the house used and, if possible, to sell them some of the products she carried in her suitcase.

On asking the question, she got some very strange replies – particularly at a fisherman's cottage near Yarmouth. She said to the fisherman's wife, 'I'm from the Family Planning Company. May I ask what method of contraception you use?'

'What do you mean?' said the lady.

'I mean, do you use the lunar method or the condom?'

The fishwife replied, 'Oh, we don't bother with none o'that! We use a herring box. My husband's much shorter than I am, so I stand 'im on the box an', when his eyes go funny, I kick the box away.'

80

★ Fun in the Park ★

The famous Shakespearian actor, Robert Atkins, for many years produced the summer productions in Regent's Park. They were all Shakespearian plays.

Casting for *Twelfth Night*, a very inexperienced student convinced him that she could play the part of Maria opposite his Sir Toby Belch. And the great man fell for it.

On the opening night she was so nervous, she failed to come on. He struggled on trying to play both parts.

At the end of the play as he was striding towards his dressing room, he noticed this crestfallen figure under a bush, sitting with her head between her knees. He said, 'It's no good looking up your entrance, you've just missed it!'

★ ★ ★

The Matinée

Actors as a rule do not like Matinées – but they have to do them – even leading ladies have to. This particular leading lady was performing at the Aldwych theatre in London and had decided to stay in the Theatre between the 'mutiny', as she called it, and the evening performance. Some food was sent in.

Later, when the call boy knocked on the door, the door flew open to reveal the actress lying on her back on the *chaise-longue* covered with nothing but a gentleman, whose shirt tails were flying.

Undaunted, she said to the call boy: 'Hello Tommy, . . . have you met my doctor?'

Behind Yer!

⋆ Behind Yer! ⋆

Some sorts of traditional pantomime can, with experienced performers, be staged very, very quickly. Through the years, funny little theatrical companies have sprung up at Christmas time to raise a bit of dosh.

Some very small outfits could only afford three or four days' rehearsal. All the panto gags would be wheeled out and adjusted into practically any popular pantomime story.

One company, with one day to go before opening, had not yet bought their red hood for *Little Red Riding Hood*. They had postponed buying the red material several times for financial reasons.

An hour before 'curtain up' the wardrobe mistress said to the producer:

'We still haven't got a hood. What shall we do?'

The producer said, 'Nip down to the stationer's and buy some red crêpe paper.'

In a few minutes – very out of breath – she returned to say the stationer's hadn't any red paper. The producer said, 'Never mind! Let's do *Cinderella*.'

Buttons

My favourite part in pantomime is Buttons in *Cinderella*.

This little scene was fun to do.

Everyone's gone to the ball except poor Cinderella, and Buttons of course, who's the serving boy.

They're sitting on the kitchen table together commiserating.

BUTTONS: Don't cry Cinderella . . . don't cry, you're making me thirsty.
(*Cinderella cries louder*)

BUTTONS: (*Producing an apple*) Here, you can have a bite o'my apple.

CINDERS: (*Brightening*) Ooh thanks! (She snatches it out of his hand and takes a big bite).

BUTTONS: (*Watching her eat the apple, enviously*) I love you Cinderella.

CINDERS: (*Startled*) I like you, but I don't love you.

BUTTONS: You don't love me?

CINDERS: No.

BUTTONS: Well, give me my apple back.

(*He snatches it back, Cinderella cries even louder*)

BUTTONS: Oh do shut up, you're not the only one that's sad. I get lonely and sad. Thank heavens I've got my goldfish to keep me company.

CINDERS: I didn't know you had goldfish.

BUTTONS: Yes.

CINDERS: How many have you got?

BUTTONS: 76.

CINDERS: 76? Where d'you keep them all?

BUTTONS: In the bath!

CINDERS: What happens if you want to take a bath?

BUTTONS: I blindfold them.

CINDERS: What would happen if I wanted to take a bath?

BUTTONS: I'd blindfold you, . . . I don't want you to see my goldfish.

(*Cinderella starts to sob again*)

BUTTONS: Oh cheer up. I tell you what, I'll make something out of this newspaper. What would you like me to make?

CINDERS: A working model of Tower Bridge.

BUTTONS: (*Pause*) . . . I think I'll make a pig.

CINDERS: No, . . . A working model of Tower Bridge.

BUTTONS: No, I think I'll make a pig.

CINDERS: (*Angrily*) *I want a working model of Tower Bridge.*

BUTTONS: All right. I'll make you a working model of Tower Bridge. *But it'll look rather like a pig.* While I'm making it, you get the children to sing 'London Bridge Is Falling Down'.

CINDERS: OK.

(*He proceeds to make a working model of Tower Bridge out of this piece of newspaper while Cinders sings with the children. He makes a right hash of it and ends up tearing it into little pieces of paper and throwing them all over the floor*)

CINDERS: You haven't made a pig!

BUTTONS: *No, . . . I've made a litter!*

★ ★ ★

Disaster

During one such production of *Cinderella* my friend Lucy Winters was playing the name part.

She developed a serious cold, very very bad, she could hardly speak. I was worried and sent for the theatre doctor who gave her an injection which made her rather woozy.

I was listening to the tannoy in the dressing room rather anxiously, when I heard Lucy Winters as Cinderella saying, 'But Fairy Godmother, . . . I can't possibly go to the rag in these balls!'

Peter Pan

During the 1930s, two productions of *Peter Pan* were produced every year. One company stayed in London and the other went on tour.

The parts of Mr Darling and Captain Hook were usually played by the same actor for financial reasons, and Nana the dog was usually played by some little acrobat.

Cecil King, the producer of the shows, was sitting in an actors' pub in theatre land, when an old actor came up to him and said, 'How's the tour going Cecil?'

He said, 'Terrible old boy! The Lost Boys are smoking in the Pirate scene, Wendy's having an affair with Captain Hook, and to top everything, Nana's got the clap!'

Backstage

Backstage drama has often been a useful theme for giant Hollywood films and theatre musicals all over the world.

Backstage of the Theatre Royal, during the second half of *Sleeping Beauty*. A seven-year-old tiny tot dressed as a fairy is sobbing her heart out.

STAGE MANAGER:	Why are you crying Mavis?
MAVIS:	Mr Brown, we won't be able to do the Woodland Ballet this afternoon.
STAGE MANAGER:	Why not Mavis?
MAVIS:	Appleblossom's shit herself.

★ ★ ★

Name Droppings

Cool

A deeply aristocratic lady said to Augustus John at one of his exhibitions:

'Do you do nude painting?'

He replied, 'Always dear Lady – but I like to keep my socks on. It's somewhere to keep the brushes!'

Groucho on Form

Groucho came to England to record a television interview programme for Lew Grade.

Groucho asked one interviewee, 'What is your profession Sir?'

The rather nervous answer was, 'I'm a tree surgeon.'

Groucho said, 'Oh, ... been up any patients lately?'

A Beecham Pill

Sir Thomas Beecham was feeding the pigeons in Trafalgar Square one day when a student carrying a violin said to him:

'Excuse me Sir, how do I get to the Albert Hall?'

Sir Thomas replied: 'Practise eight hours a day!'

The great Sir Thomas, in his early days, would sometimes conduct amateur orchestras but taking with him, for professional support, the leader of his orchestra.

One day, Sir Thomas was conducting with his usual brio when he noticed the orchestra was losing the struggle to keep up with him. Still conducting, he leant forward and whispered conspiratorially to his leader, 'Don't look now but I think we're being followed!'

★ ★ ★

Noël Coward was asked to perform in a big charity show at the London Coliseum. As this was an annual event, Noël asked the organisers what they were going to call the show this year.

They said, 'Summer Stars.'

He said, 'Yes – and some're not!'

I heard the other day that Noël Coward was once looking at the cast list for a famous film called *The Sea Shall Not Have Them*, and he said, 'Why not, everybody else has!'

David Niven

David Niven lived in Monaco and was great friends with Prince Rainier but they had a falling out and didn't speak for some months. One day Prince Rainier rang Niven up and said it was too silly being in this small place and not being friends so they agreed to meet at their favourite restaurant for a reconciliation dinner.

All went well and they had a delicious meal, lots of wine and cigars. After their third glass of brandy Prince Rainier leant over the table confidentially and said to Niven, 'David, I know when you were in Hollywood you were a great one with the ladies and slept with just about everyone; just which of the actresses you took to bed would you say was the best?'

Niven, slightly the worse for wear, said, 'No question about it: Grace . . . um! . . . Gracie Fields.'

★ ★ ★

Stage Direction

I heard that Sir John Gielgud, a gentleman if ever there was one, was having great difficulty directing a certain actor at rehearsals. The opening night was fast approaching and Sir John went home rather desperate to tell his friend about the awkward actor.

His friend responded with this advice: 'If he starts again tomorrow be strong and just tell him to fuck off.'

Came the next day, rehearsals went with a swing when just before lunch break the actor started again. Long-winded questions on motivations and such like. Sir John sprang up from his seat and ran down to the front of the dress circle shouting, 'Oh fuck away! fuck away!'

Amazing Grace

George Burns said to Gracie, 'Did your maid drop you on your head when you were a baby?'

Gracie said, 'Don't be silly, we couldn't afford a maid, . . . My mother had to do it.'

Cliff Michelmore

When it was first suggested that teenagers should have the vote at eighteen, Cliff Michelmore, the interviewer, was sent out by the BBC to ask what the public thought of this suggestion.

He went to a bus queue, and as a lady was getting on the bus he asked her this question: 'Do you think teenagers should have the vote?'

'Well,' she said, 'they stay at school 'til they're much longer now, don't they?'

Animal Attraction

*Some people prefer animals
to human beings.
I wonder if animals do!*

★ ★ ★

Have a Nice One

Alistair, aged eleven, was fishing in the loch, when a local policeman came upon him and remarked, 'It's an awfu' naice dee furr fishin.'

Alistair said, 'Aye.'

The policeman said, 'Why'rre ye not at school?'

Alistair said, 'Like ye said, it's an awfu' naice dee furr fishin.'

Keep Right On . . .

An old tramp was trudging along, lonely and dejected.

Suddenly he came across a little frog in his path – he tried to walk round it but the frog hopped always in his way.

He bent down with great difficulty when the frog chirped up, 'Give us a kiss and and I will turn into a beautiful girl, then you can take me home and make love to me.'

The tramp put the frog in his side pocket and trudged on; three minutes later there was a commotion in his pocket – he took the frog out and once again the frog said, 'Kiss me and I will turn into a beautiful girl, then you can take me home and make love to me.'

The tramp said, 'Thanks for the offer, but the way I feel at the moment I'd sooner have a talking frog.'

 A Ducking

By the side of the lake in St James's Park, London, a hungry old tramp snatched a duck from the water and quickly started to pluck it. A policeman nearby startled him and he chucked the nearly naked duck back on the water. As it swam around, the policeman, seeing the pile of feathers said, 'What's going on here?'

And the tramp said quick as a flash, 'Well, he's having a swim, and I'm minding his clothes.'

A small dog fell into a rock pool on the coast of Malta. The waves were pretty high and he couldn't get out of the pool.

A Jewish gentleman jumped in and got the dog out to safety. He started to give the dog artificial respiration and mouth to mouth resuscitation. A bystander said, 'My goodness, you're a brave man Sir. Are you a vet?'

The man said, 'Vet – I'm bloody soaking!'

 Country Life

Two people living in the country went to a fancy dress party dressed as a cow and won the first prize. Naturally they drank plenty and were just going home when they saw it was pouring with rain.

They decided to put the cow skin on again to keep dry, and as they staggered home across the fields, the wife, who was in the back half, looked through a hole in the skin and saw farmer Giles' bull following. She shrieked in terror:

'Farmer's big bull's following us. What shall we do?'

Her nice, kind husband shouted back, 'I'm going to run like hell, you'll just have to make your own arrangements!'

Standing early one evening near Olympia where the famous Dog Show, Crufts, had been held, were two owners. One of them said, 'How did your dog get on?'

The other said, 'Very good. Two "Firsts", two "Seconds" and a "Highly Commended". How did your dog get on?'

And the first owner said, 'Great . . . two bites, two bonks and highly delighted!'

Good Dog

Two golfers were talking, and one of them said:

'I wish they'd let me take my dog on this golf course, he's really clever, he performs beautifully, he loves going golfing.'

The other golfer said, 'Why, what does he do?'

He said, 'Well, when I hit a good drive he sits up and begs and bangs his forepaws together.'

The other man said, 'Supposing you do a duff shot that goes in the rough, what does he do then?'

He said, 'Well, he does somersaults.'

The other man said, 'Why does he do somersaults?'

He said, 'I kick him up the behind.'

Discipline

A guide dog was leading a blind man across the road, mistimed it, and they were nearly run over by a big bus. When they got to the other side of the road, the blind man stooped down and gave the dog a sweet. A bystander who saw this said, 'You're a good, kind man. Instead of punishing the dog, you gave it a sweet.'

The man said, 'I had to find out where his mouth was, so I could kick his bum!'

Good Question

A crocodile went into a pub and sat down at the bar.
The barman said, 'So why the long face?'

You can get locked up for this sort of thing!

Triumph

A very excited, ancient gentleman, went into a Catholic church to confess.

'Father,' he said, 'I am eighty-seven years old, I met a young woman last night and took her home, and we made love eight times.'

The priest said, 'What is your name my son?'

He said, 'Simon Feldman.'

The priest said, 'Oh, shouldn't you be telling this to somebody else?'

And Simon said, 'I'm telling everyone!'

A boy and girl were standing in a doorway rather late at night when she started to cry. He said, 'Why're you crying?'

She said, 'I've got to go home and tell my mother I've been naughty twice tonight.'

He said, 'What do you mean twice? You're not going home yet are you?'

Snubbed

One day, a man realised a life-long ambition, and bought himself a beautiful pair of snakeskin shoes.

When he went home he walked up and down in front of his wife hoping she would notice how beautiful the shoes were. She ignored the whole performance.

During the evening, he used various ruses to draw her attention to the shoes. Even putting his feet up on the table. But to no avail! When they went to bed, he got into his pyjamas, but left his snakeskin shoes on. She didn't notice! In desperation he took his pyjamas off leaving the shoes on. There he was, stark naked, walking up and down the bedroom and then he eventually went and stood in front of her and said, 'Don't you notice anything different?'

She looked him up and down and said, 'No – everything's about the same. It's still dangling down.'

He said, 'It is not dangling – it's pointing towards my new snakeskin shoes!'

She said, 'Oh really, it's a pity you didn't buy a new hat!'

A New Angle

I used to go fishing with a friend and he was always lucky.

Whichever side of the boat he sat he always caught a lot of fish and I seemed to catch very little if any.

I said, 'How is this?'

He said, 'Well, in the morning, when I wake up, if the wife's asleep on the right-hand side, I fish on the right-hand side of the boat. If she's lying on her left-hand side, I fish on the left-hand side of the boat and it seems to work.'

I said, 'Great, but what happens if she's lying on her back?'

He said, 'I don't go fishing.'

How Sad

A rather aged man was sitting on a park bench crying his eyes out, and a man came and sat next to him, and asked him why he was sobbing so.

He said, 'Well, I lost my wife three years ago.'

The man said, 'Oh, I am sorry.'

The old chap said, 'But I was so lonely, I hired a housekeeper, and she's a beautiful woman, and so nice and sweet. We married and we have a wonderful sex life. We make love nearly three times a week.'

And the man said, 'Good, congratulations, but why're you crying?'

He said, 'I can't remember where I live.'

Dear Doctor

The Doctor said to ancient Mr Brown, 'What can I do for you this morning?'

Mr Brown said, 'I would like a sperm count please Doctor.'

The Doctor said, 'Why do you want a sperm count at your age?'

Mr Brown said, 'I'm only ninety-four! And I'm getting married on Friday. And my bride-to-be wants me to have a sperm count.'

The Doctor said, 'How old is your bride-to-be?'

He said, 'She's only eighty-seven – and she's very fond of me.'

The Doctor said, 'Very well Mr Brown. Take this bottle and do your best, and I'll see you in a couple of days' time. Good morning.'

Three weeks later, the Doctor met Mr Brown in the village and said, 'How're you getting on with . . . you know?'

And Mr Brown said, 'Not at all well Doctor. She tried it with her right hand, she tried it with her left hand, she tried it with her teeth in, she tried it with her teeth out – and we still can't get the top off the bottle!'

FIRST MAN: We had burglars last night. I think they must've been gay.

SECOND MAN: Why d'you think they were gay?

FIRST MAN: Well, the furniture'd been rearranged and they'd left a quiche in the oven!

Modesty

A nun was having a bath, as nuns do, when there came a knock on the door.

She said, 'Oooh, don't come in.'

A voice said, 'It's all right – Blind man.'

She said, 'All right, you can come in.'

When he went in he said, 'Lovely tits – now where d'you want this blind?'

Gemütlich

At an annual fair in a remote mountain village in Austria, one of the many attractions was a gypsy with a performing bear. At the end of the day, feeling sorry for the gypsy, a wealthy farmer who'd imbibed rather a lot of wine, invited him and his bear back to the farm to sleep.

The farmer's wife was very angry, and said, 'They'll have to sleep in the attic with Helga, the serving girl. She's very polite, and she won't mind.'

At two o'clock in the morning the man crept over to Helga and said, 'How about a bit of fun?'

She said, 'Go away – the gentleman in the fur coat's been over twice!'

Midnight Choo Choo

Third-class sleepers in London to Glasgow night trains used to contain four bunks, two up and two down. They were often occupied by people who'd never met before. One gent, who'd bought his wife an ironing board as a present, climbed up and put the ironing board beside him out of the way. He noticed later a very pretty girl in the opposite bunk. When the lights were dimmed, he whispered, 'How about a bunk up?'

She whispered back, 'OK. But how're you going to get across without disturbing the people in the bunks below?'

Remembering the ironing board, he whispered, 'I've got something here that will stretch across and I can climb along it.'

A voice from the bunk below said, 'Congratulations – but how're you going to get back?'

Who do you think you're kidding?

Bad Times

Bad times produced good jokes, and World War II was a very bad time, with food shortages. Many foods had to be rationed.

Hence, Mrs Pringle went to the grocer's shop, queued up for half an hour, got so tired she leaned against the bacon slicer, *and got behind with her bacon ration*!

Rather distressed, she went off in quite a hurry to the fishmonger, and queued up. When she got to the counter, she said to the fishmonger, 'Half a pound of cod please.'

He said, 'Sorry Madam, we haven't got any cod.'

She said, 'Yes you have. You've got some under the counter.'

He said, 'Madam, we have not got any cod!'

She didn't believe him, so she went and stood at the back of the queue again, and as she got to the counter, she said, 'Half a pound of cod please.'

He said, 'Madam, I've just told you there is no cod!'

She said, 'I bet you've got some hidden under the counter.'

He said, 'Listen Lady. How many H's in hake?'
She said, 'One.'
He said, 'Then how many F's in cod?'
She said, 'There's no F in cod.'
He said, *'That's what I keep trying to tell you!'*

... to be Kind

An old butcher I know called Jack Jones was telling me the other day that during the 1914/18 war young boys just out of school were given a little bit of training and sent up to the front.

One young soldier he knew brought a prisoner back to headquarters. When he arrived, he said to the Officer, 'Reporting with prisoner of war Sir.'

This particular officer was so rich he could hardly speak! But he managed to make some noises, which were intended to mean, 'Where is the prisoner then?'

The young soldier said, 'I haven't got him with me Sir.'

The Officer went very red in the face and managed to blurt out, 'What causes this?'

The private said, 'Well, we was marching along, I was behind him with fixed bayonet, as told to by the Sergeant Sir, and I was not fraternising with him at all. But he started fraternising with me, and kept on about how awfully sad he was because he could not see his family again, for years and years, and his children, an' that. And he started to cry, and I started to cry, so I shot the poor bugger to put him out of his misery!'

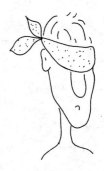

Before World War II, during one of Winston Churchill's spells of unemployment, he came across a gardener he had not seen before in the grounds of Chartwell. 'How long have you worked for me?' asked Churchill.

'Nearly five years, Sir,' he answered almost pulling his forelock off.

'Splendid!' said Mr Churchill. 'Are you a married man?'

'Yes Sir, with fourteen children.'

'That's a lot of children,' remarked Churchill.

'I know Sir,' said the gardener, 'but I'm very fond of my wife.'

'Well,' said Mr Churchill. 'I'm fond of a cigar, but I take it out sometimes!'

Silly Cow

During World War II, many unlikely people were drafted to work on the land.

Two old cows were talking in a field as cows do. The first cow said, 'There are such funny people milking us these days.'

The second cow said, 'I know my dear. Yesterday I had a ladies hairdresser milking me. Such a delicate touch; sent a thrill right through my cheddar gorge.'

The first cow said, 'You're lucky. I got the bell ringer from the cathedral!'

Welsh Wales

At the end of World War II, 'black outs' were deemed no longer necessary. Some little Welsh villages were rather slow in cancelling the order, so that when the pubs turned out, the streets were still in darkness.

The young couples would pair off and drift romantically into the Welsh hills.

One night the following was heard as the pub emptied:

VOICE IN THE DISTANCE: Dai?
DAI: (*Shouting*) What is it Ian?'
IAN: D'you mind swapping –
I've got my sister again.

Have you heard the one about...?

Have you heard the one about the MP who dreamt he was making a speech in parliament, woke up and found he was?

The ex-prime minister, Margaret Thatcher, was called away from a book-signing engagement in order to meet some old-age pensioners in their newly built home.

Shaking hands with one old man, she said, 'Do you know who I am?'

He replied, 'No – but if you go to the reception, they may be able to tell you.'

Coincidence

Two ladies, Alice and Gladys, were sitting on a park bench feeding the pigeons.

Alice said, 'I've had three husbands and they're all dead!'

Gladys said, 'Ooh, that's sad, what happened?'

She said, 'The first one died of eating dodgy mushrooms.'

Gladys said, 'How terrible. What happened to the second one?'

Alice said, 'You're never going to believe this . . . it's such a coincidence. But he died of dodgy mushrooms too.'

Gladys said, 'What on earth happened to the third one?'

She said, 'Concussion.'

Gladys said, 'Really?'

She said, 'Yes – I had to hit 'im on the head with a mallet.'

Gladys said, 'Why?'

Alice said, 'He wouldn't eat his mushrooms!'

Cheerful

I went round to see a friend of mine yesterday who'd just died. And I said to his wife, 'He's got a lovely tan on him, hasn't he?'

She said, 'Well, that weekend in Worthing did him the world of good.'

I said, 'And look at the smile, what a lovely smile on his face!'

She said, 'Well, that's not surprising – he died in 'is sleep. He don't know he's dead yet!'

Contentment

This little boy was the son of very wealthy parents. By the age of three, he hadn't uttered a sound. They took him to many specialists. By the age of five he still hadn't said anything, and was now costing them a fortune for voice therapists. On his seventh birthday he said, 'These kippers are far too salty!'

Totally flabbergasted they said to him:

'What on earth stopped you talking to us before? We've spent a fortune on you. Why didn't you speak?'

He said, 'Well, everything's been all right up to now.'

Organic

A man visiting Fortnum & Mason, had heard that the staff of the most exclusive grocer's shop in the world always behaved and dressed impeccably.

On arrival at the magnificent entrance, he entered, and a man in a tail coat said, 'Can I help you Sir?'

The customer said, 'Er ... I'd like a pound of tomatoes please.'

'Certainly Sir,' said the supervisor, 'This way if you please.'

On receiving the tomatoes, he said, 'How much?'

'Six pounds and fifty pence,' said the supervisor.

The customer was very shaken, handed the tomatoes back and said, 'Six pounds fifty! You know what you can do with them, don't you?'

And the supervisor said, 'Yes Sir. But at the moment I'm having some difficulty accommodating a 3 lb cucumber!'

At the Station

While waiting for their train, two men were having a glass of lager in a British Rail restaurant. One of them noticed a gentleman in black with a red waistcoat, reading *The Times* newspaper. And he said to his mate, 'Look over in that corner, I think it's the Archbishop of Canterbury.'

The man looked and said, 'No . . . 'course it isn't.'

The first one said, 'I'll bet it is. I know it is! He's got a red waistcoat. I'll bet you a fiver it's the Archbishop of Canterbury.'

So his friend said, 'OK, you're on for a fiver. Now go and ask him.'

He went over and said to the man 'Excuse me Sir – are you the Archbishop of Canterbury?'

The man replied, 'Oh, piss off.'

He went back to his beer slightly cross-eyed. His friend said, 'Well, is he the Archbishop of Canterbury?'

He said, 'Don't know – wouldn't say.'

Out of Court

A courtroom in East Anglia. The cowman has a thick country accent.

CLERK OF THE COURT:	The next witness wishes to make a request Your Honour.
CIRCUIT JUDGE:	Certainly.
COW MAN:	Permission to make a request of Your Honour?
CIRCUIT JUDGE:	Proceed Mr Haycroft.
COW MAN:	I request of Your Honour, that I do not have to attend court this afternoon Sir.
CIRCUIT JUDGE:	For what reason?
COW MAN:	My wife's expecting a conception Your Honour.
CIRCUIT JUDGE:	Well, I'm not quite sure what you mean, but I feel you should be there.

★ ★ ★

Service with a Smile

At the beginning of the holiday season the staff in a hotel are all sweetness and light. At the end of the season there's a slightly different story. Here's the story:

A not amazingly good-looking, overweight lady goes to the counter and says, 'I want the complaints department.'

The girl behind the reception desk says, 'We haven't got one, you big fat pig!'

#

When it snowed, the boys and girls came out to play, but we were a poor family. We couldn't afford a toboggan – I had to slide down on my cousin.

We were so poor I didn't have any clothes till I was seven. And on my seventh birthday, me Auntie put a hat on me and said, 'Now you can look out of the window.'

A friend of mine named Jackie, was guiding some American tourists around Runnymede, and one of the tourists said, 'Jackie, when was the Magna Carta signed?'

Jackie replied, 'Twelve fifteen.'

And the lady, looking at her watch, said, 'Oh Gosh, we just missed it.'

Hair Raising

A man sat down on a hairdresser's chair and said, 'Shampoo and cut please.'

The hairdresser said, 'Would you mind removing your hat please.'

The gentleman said, 'Ooh, sorry.' Revealing only three hairs.

After a brief shampoo, the hairdresser said, 'How would you like it Sir?'

'Short back and sides and parted on the left,' said the man.

As he went to comply, one of the hairs fell out, leaving only two hairs. The hairdresser said, 'Oh dear. What shall we do Sir?'

The man said, 'No problem – part them in the middle.'

Just as the hairdresser started, yet another hair fell out. The crimper, now horrified at the sight of only one hair said, 'Good God Sir, now what can we do?'

The man said, 'Oh, never mind. Just leave it messy.'

★ ★ ★

Helpful

A man queuing up at the reception of a hotel in the southern hemisphere said to his neighbour, 'Excuse me Sir, is this pronounced Hawaii or Havaii?'

The other man said, 'Havaii.'

He said, 'Thank you.'

The other replied, 'You're velcome.'

Stormy Weather

A man and a woman were having the usual exciting breakfast conversation about whether it was going to rain or not, and should he take his umbrella to work. He decided it was going to be fine, kissed his wife goodbye, and left.

A few minutes later, the milkman came through the back door, and was immediately in a close embrace with the lady. The milkman and the lady kissed passionately as the rain started to patter against the window.

'Whose beautiful eyes are these darling?' said the milkman.

'Yours darling,' said the lady.

'And whose little mouth is this?' said the milkman.

'Yours darling,' she said.

'And whose little nose is this?' said the milkman.

The husband rushed in very wet and said, 'When you come to the umbrella, it's mine!'

Hope Springs . . .

He was ninety-three and she was eighty-nine and they married. They spent their honeymoon getting into the taxi!

Christmas is Coming...

Just before last Christmas, a dustman was clattering away at the back of a lady's house when she opened the kitchen door and said, 'Good morning dustman. Do come in – I've made you a nice breakfast.'

The surprised dustman went inside and polished off the meal and said, 'Thank you very much Madam. You're very kind.'

She said, 'That's nothing, come up to the bedroom, I've got something else for you.'

Now totally bewitched, he followed her upstairs. They both fell on to the bed and had a great time. Afterwards, she handed him a pound note. Reluctantly snatching it out of her hand he said, 'This is too much. You have already given me the best Christmas box I've ever had.'

She said, 'Well, it's what my husband wanted.'

He said, 'Your old man?'

She said, 'Yes. When I told him I'd given the postman and the milkman their Christmas presents but wasn't sure about you, he said, "Oh screw the dustman, give him a pound!" – but the breakfast was my idea.'

Ambition

A rather simple but lovable public lavatory attendant in a small town in the north of England had a burning ambition to be in charge of a public 'Gents' in central London, rather like an actor wanting to play the Theatre Royal, Drury Lane.

He saved up and travelled by train the long journey to the Metropolis. On arrival at King's Cross Station he walked all the way to Leicester Square and much to his joy, came across the Gents right in the centre of what was once the British Empire.

As he walked in wonderment down to the bowels (if you'll forgive the expression) of Leicester Square, sweet notes such as Handel's Water Music rang in his ears. But alas, it was in reality, running water from the urinal.

He addressed as if to royalty, the old attendant who was mopping the floor, explaining his ambition to work in what was to him the hub of the Universe, whereupon the kindly old attendant said, 'It's not like that at all son. It's mostly 'orrible down 'ere. You get terrible types who get up to all sorts, injecting themselves and sniffing that powder stuff. If anyone comes in for a straight crap, it's like a breath of fresh air!'

A scrap metal merchant knocked on the gates of Heaven. Saint Peter came to the gates and said, 'What is your profession?'

The man said, 'I was a scrap metal merchant.'

Saint Peter said, 'I'm not sure about that. I'd better go and ask.'

He went away – *and when he came back the gates had gone!*

The Boyfriend

A rather posh lady took her scrap-metal-merchant boyfriend to the Savoy Grill. It was the first time he'd been in an up-market restaurant.

When the head waiter came round and asked him if he would like something off the trolley he said, 'Yes . . . I'll have the wheels.'

Language

A Hungarian gentleman who could speak not a word of English, was obliged to go to London. He said to his friend, 'What on earth can I order when I go in a restaurant?'

And his friend said, 'Just say, fish and chips, and you'll be all right.'

After a week of eating fish and chips, he got desperate and rang up his friend in Hungary.

'I'm sick of that, what else can I ask for?'

His friend said, 'Say, roast beef.'

At the next meal, the waiter said, 'What can I get you?'

The Hungarian said, 'Roast beef.'

And the waiter said, 'Certainly Sir. Well done or under done?'

The Hungarian said, 'Fish and chips.'

Robin Hood, the well-known 'do-gooder', was very seriously wounded during a battle outside Nottingham Castle. His Merry Men dragged him off and hid him in a very small shepherd's cottage.

As he lay dying they said to him, 'Speak to us Robin, speak to us.'

He said, 'Give me my bow and arrow, and where the arrow falls, bury me.'

So he shot an arrow – and they buried him on top of the wardrobe!

 The Cafe

A rather depressed man who'd just been made redundant, went into a seedy little cafe, with a seedy old waiter serving.

The waiter who was very short-sighted was dusting round the tables and dusted the man as well, who said, 'What are you doing?'

The waiter said, 'Sorry Sir, What can I get you?'

He said, 'I want a boiled egg, a plate of bread and butter and a pot of tea . . . and a few kind words.'

'Very good Sir,' said the old waiter, writing it down.

'A boiled egg . . . a plate of bread and butter . . . and a pot of tea.'

'Don't forget the few . . .'

'No, I know Sir . . . a few kind words.'

He went out and came back about quarter of an hour later. He said, 'There we are Sir. A boiled egg, a plate of bread and butter, and a pot of tea.'

The man said, 'What about the few kind words?'

The waiter said, 'Oh yes Sir . . . Don't eat the egg.'

Prejudice

Probably the most idiotic form of prejudice is that against black people.

Not long after World War II finished, many immigrants came to live in the so-called United Kingdom.

Owners of bars and such were inclined to put a notice on their wall which read NO COLOUREDS, which was intended to please the regular customers, and it did.

One morning a pub owner was opening his pub, and in came a newly arrived man from Pakistan. Before he had a chance to say 'Out', the Pakistani said, 'I am hearing that Guinness is good for you, one glass please.'

The publican, in an effort to dissuade said, 'That'll be three pounds.'

In his ignorance of the real price he paid up happily.

The next morning he turned up again with twenty friends and again paid the outrageous price. The barman was serving them happily, when in walked a British road mender who said, 'I thought you had a colour bar here?'

And the publican said, 'I have . . . piss off!'

A skeleton walks into a public house and says to the barman, 'A pint of lager please – and a mop.'

Beware

Have you heard about the Gay Mafia?
They come round
and criticise your curtains!

Partnership

Not that long ago, it was not uncommon to see a blind man selling matches from a tray. A little sign on the tray read, 'Blind'. It encouraged people to put money in the tray – people seldom took the matches.

This is how the old joke goes:

Yesterday I went to put sixpence in a blind man's tin, but missed it, and the sixpence fell on to the pavement. The blind man stooped down and put it in his tin. I said, 'That's a funny thing for a blind man to do!'

He said, 'Oh, I'm not blind governor – I'm just standing in for my friend.'

I said, 'Where's your friend?'

He said, 'He's in the cinema watching *Ben Hur*.'

Happy Ending

Two old widowers living together suffered from short-term loss of memory. One afternoon, the following ensued:

BILL: Ben, while you're in the village, get me a vanilla ice-cream cornet will you?

BEN: OK.

BILL: You won't forget will you?

BEN: (*Ten yards down the road*) 'Course not!

BILL: And Ben – ask them to stick a chocolate flake in it, will you?

BEN: (*Now twenty-five yards down the road, shouting*) . . . OhhKaay.

BILL: (*Bawling*) Ben?

BEN: What now?

BILL: Get them to pour some hundreds and thousands on the top please.

BEN: (*In the distance*) . . . OhhKaay.

BILL: Don't forgeeet . . .

Later, Ben appears in the kitchen, a little out of breath, carrying a hamburger.

BEN: There you are Bill.

BILL: Where's the chips?

Package Deal

A cannibal returned from a package holiday, and his friend said, 'Did you enjoy yourself?'

He said, 'Yes.'

His friend said, 'Where's your left arm?'

He said, 'Well – it was self-catering.'

God Save the Queen

Since Queen Elizabeth II has thrown open the doors of Buckingham Palace to the public, there's been some confusion in the Guardroom. For instance, The Guard commander said to a rather dim recruit one night, 'Now listen Private, when you're on guard tonight, remember . . . there're impostors about. So for gawd's sake make sure they know who they think they are . . . Right!'

Guarding the Palace was one thing, actually having to think about it was another.

At 3 a.m. that morning, the poor young private said to a shadowy figure, 'Halt. Who goes there?'

A voice answered, 'Army Chaplain.'

Not believing him the soldier said, 'Halt. Who goes there?'

There came the same answer, 'Army Chaplain.'

And then the third time, the soldier, very nervous, said, 'Halt or I fire.'

And the voice said, 'Don't be stupid.'

So the soldier shot him, walked over, felt the body with his boots and said, 'Bloody Charlie Chaplin!'

★ ★ ★

Just Testing

A lady was driving home with a friend, having just failed her third driving test. She saw two men working up a telegraph pole, and she shouted, 'Stupid idiots, what are they doing up there? . . . My driving's not that bad!'

Two very drunk fellows left a pub one night, and staggered home the short cut, straight along the railway line.

One of them said, 'These stairs are a bit steep!'

And the other one said, 'Yes, . . . and the banisters are too low . . . '

Every Cloud...

Rachel said to her daughter, 'How's your marriage going daughter?'

She said, 'Things are desperate mother. He's being an absolute swine. He never speaks to the children, he gets up late. When he goes out I know he goes with other women, and what money we have he's spending on the horses. It's terrible, I'm losing weight so fast, I've lost six or seven kilos already . . . '

Rachel said, 'You'll have to divorce him.'

The daughter said, 'I'm going to, I'm going to. Not yet though . . . I want to lose another two kilos.'

Good Luck

A man goes to visit his friend in hospital. When he gets in the ward he sees he's smothered from head to foot in bandages.

'What happened?' he said.

'I went through a plate glass window,' said the man.

The other chap said, 'Good job you were wearing those bandages.'

These days charity is apparently the backbone of the country. They came knocking on my door yesterday collecting for the old people's home – so I gave them my father!

Or do you prefer this?

They came knocking at my door yesterday collecting for the new swimming pool – so I gave them a bucket of water!

Heavenly

A man was trying to get entrance into Heaven. Saint Peter was asking him all the various questions, and there seemed to be some difficulty.

And Saint Peter said, 'You can only come to heaven if you've led a good life. Did you smoke?'

And the man said, 'Yes.'

He said, 'How many?'

He said, 'About sixty a day.'

Saint Peter said, 'Did you drink?'

He said, 'Yes.'

'A lot?'

'Yes. I drank as much as I could.'

Saint Peter said, 'You're not being very helpful – isn't there anything decent you did in your life?'

So he said, 'Oh yes, . . . yes. I went to help a girl who was being beaten up and mugged by an armed gang.'

Saint Peter said, 'That sounds better. When did this happen?'

The man said, 'About three minutes ago!'

A Christian girl was going to marry a Jewish fellow. So she went to the Rabbi to find out the correct rules. The Rabbi said, 'The man you're going to marry is strictly orthodox. You must not dance with him at the wedding. Do you hear – do not dance with him at the wedding.'

'When the marriage is consummated,' said the girl, 'will the man be on top?'

'That would be OK,' said the Rabbi.

'May the woman be on top?'

'That would be allowed also,' said the Rabbi.

'How about standing up?' said the girl.

'Definitely not,' said the Rabbi. 'That might lead to dancing.'

Another Chance

The secretary in a private hospital was talking to the boss man about a patient who'd been given six months to live.

She said, 'The six months is nearly up Sir, and he can't pay the bill.'

The boss said, 'Well, give 'im another six months!'

Honestly

Many years ago, the Captain of an ocean-going steamer needed some deckhands to mop the decks. He said to one applicant, 'What's your name?'

'Murphy Sir,' said the man.

'Have you done this sort of work before?'

'Yes Sir, many times.'

'Are you a married man?' said the Captain.

'Oh yes, Sir. Very very married. I married a lovely girl and we have tirteen children.'

'Have you sent them all to school?'

'Oh yes, Sir. They've all been very highly educated.'

'Are you a diligent worker Murphy?'

'Oh yes Sir,' said Murphy. 'Very very diligent Sir.'

'OK, you've got the job,' said the Captain.

'Thank you very much Sir,' said Murphy.

The next applicant's name was Smith and the Captain said, 'Have you done this sort of work before Smith?'

'Yes Sir, I have.'

'Are you a married man?'

'Yes Sir, I am.'

'Any children?'

'Yes Sir, I have three children.'

'OK, you've got the job,' said the Captain.

One day out at sea, Murphy said to the Captain, 'Excuse me Sir, I'd just like to ask you, when you granted this position to me Sir, you asked me many many questions before you gave me the job. And yet Smith, you only asked him three questions. What causes this Sir, what is the reason for this difference?'

The Captain said, 'Well, Smith's got an honest face.'

'Thank you very much,' said Murphy.

Three nights later there was a terrible storm, and while Murphy and Smith were mopping the decks, a great wave came up and Smith started to run. But the wave caught him up and swept him overboard.

The Captain shouted, 'What's going on down there?'

And Murphy replied, 'Well Sir, you know the one with the honest face? He's just buggered off with your mop!'

Grave News

STAGE DIRECTION: *Broad Yorkshire accent*

A man phoned an undertaker in York saying he would like *Lord She Is Thine* engraved on his wife's tombstone. The undertaker gave the work to the apprentice. Later the customer went to the grave-side and saw that an 'e' was missing, it read *Lord she is thin*. He phoned up to complain. The undertaker apologised and phoned through to the apprentice saying 'you've left the 'e' out of the work.' When the customer went back he saw it now read *Ee Lord she is thin*.

The Champion

While demolishing an old house in County Cork some builders came across a skeleton in a dark cupboard. Pinned to the skeleton's chest was a medal inscribed *Hide and Seek Champion, 1921.*

Footnote

Dear Reader

I am writing this footnote with my foot. Compiling this book has given me compiler's elbow!

Bye Bye my dears and have a nice weekend.

yours
celine x, x.

Author's Acknowledgements

Thank you to helpful incogniti and funny friends

Alex Alexander
Michael Bentine
Ronnie Corbett
Barry Cryer
Harry Fowler
Derek Lister
Spike Milligan
Priscilla Morgan
Peter Noble
David Roberts
Keith Smith
Eric Sykes
Charlie White
and
Lisa Johns
who patiently processed my words